the SE7EN DEADLY SINS *of* Writing

Common Pitfalls of Prose
...and How to Avoid Them

ANGIE KIESLING

T0098606

THE 7 DEADLY SINS OF WRITING
Common Pitfalls of Prose...and How to Avoid Them

Published in New York, New York, by Morgan James Publishing. Morgan James is a trademark of Morgan James, LLC. www. MorganJamesPublishing.com

The Morgan James Speakers Group can bring authors to your live event. For more information or to book an event visit The Morgan James Speakers Group at www.TheMorganJamesSpeakersGroup.com.

ISBN 9781683506850 paperback
ISBN 9781683506867 eBook
Library of Congress Control Number: 2017911645

Cover Design by:
Rachel Lopez
www.r2cdesign.com

Interior Design by:
Chris Treccani
www.3dogcreative.net

In an effort to support local communities, raise awareness and funds, Morgan James Publishing donates a percentage of all book sales for the life of each book to Habitat for Humanity Peninsula and Greater Williamsburg.

Get involved today! Visit www.MorganJamesBuilds.com

CONTENTS

If Writing Were Baking...

How to Use This Tiny Tome

If you were a baker, across three decades of baking you'd have seen a lot of crescent rolls, right? You'd know the recipe so well you could probably bake those rolls in your sleep.

When I hit my third decade in the publishing business as a writer and book editor, I realized I could spot most "bread-baking" mishaps at fifty paces. Maybe, just maybe, other writers might benefit from the discipline I'd learned across the years, I reasoned.

Wanting to keep things light, I borrowed a concept from the Middle Ages, likening the seven most common *pitfalls of prose* to the 7 Deadly Sins—or Don'ts, as they're referred to in this tiny book.

Tiny is a key word here because I know you're stretched for time. We all are. Quick reads are good, allowing you to get in and get out, takeaway in tow. Consider this book a list of seven things NOT to do when writing (each entry flips the title on its head so you know exactly what TO DO for best writing results—these are called Divine Do's).

If you freefall into one of the "Don'ts" the next time you sit down to write, no worries: I promise you won't wind up on a ledge in Purgatory. There's still time to redeem your prose. Every time you practice the craft of writing, your skill increases.

Notice I said craft; writing is just that. Historically speaking, it took years for a journeyman/apprentice to reach the level of a master craftsman, but you can shorten the distance as a writer by following the example of great writers. The more you *read* great writing, the better writer you will become.

A LITTLE LEAVEN, ANYONE?

As you'll soon see, most of the items in my Deadly Don'ts list are perfectly good words and phrases—even parts of speech—that every writer uses when they compose text. The key is in their usage and frequency. It's been said that "a little leaven leaveneth the whole lump"; keep that in mind as you sift through the Deadly Don'ts. For bread bakers, leaven is a necessary ingredient. But throw *too much* leaven into the mix and you'll have a big mess on your hands. The recipe requires just the right touch.

Another thing worth mentioning up front is that all writers have a distinct voice (if you haven't found your voice yet, keep writing; it will emerge over time). Some of the Deadly Don'ts may seem to imply that all writers must write the same way. Of course they don't. Good writing allows for different styles—lyrical (think Fitzgerald); punchy and staccato and lean (Hemingway); complex and psychological (Joyce Carol Oates); stream-of-consciousness (Virginia Woolf) . . . and that's only a sampling. Yet all four are revered as great writers. While their writing is fiction, the advice in this book applies to nonfiction writing as well.

It's equally true that writing changes over the course of decades and centuries, and reading tastes change too. Most readers today expect your words to work a lot harder than, say, those of an author one hundred-plus years ago. I'm guilty of this myself. As much as I love a good Dickens tale, I'd be hard-pressed to struggle through all 716 pages of *Little Dorrit*—my favorite of his stories adapted for film (miniseries), but famous for being a hard read.

My advice: take the Deadly Don'ts with a pinch of salt. The reasoning behind this little book is that I see so many manuscripts, both fiction and nonfiction, falter for the very reasons stated below. With a keen eye and a little practice, you can train yourself to turn the Deadly Don'ts into Divine Do's—and perhaps create your own test-of-time-worthy prose.

I've intentionally written this book using everyday language and refrained from stuffing it with grammar rules. If I succeeded in my goal, that approach will make it more readable.

Whether you're just starting down the road marked "WRITER" or a seasoned pro revisiting the basics, I hope *The 7 Deadly Sins of Writing* reminds you, all over again, of what makes writing so wonderful.

So here, at a glance, are the 7 Deadly Sins of Writing:

- Deadly Don't #1: Passive Voice
- Deadly Don't #2: Weak Verbs

- Deadly Don't #3: Adjective/Adverb Overload
- Deadly Don't #4: "I Began to Start..."
- Deadly Don't #5: That, That, That...
- Deadly Don't #6: There Is/Are Overload
- Deadly Don't #7: Telling vs. Showing

Are you ready to get started? Let's go!

THE DEADLY DON'TS

The best piece of advice I can give you as a writer is to learn to self-edit your work, and these 7 Deadly Sins of Writing are my top picks for how to do that. With a little practice, you can train your eye and your writing instincts to do these seven things automatically. Before too long they'll become second nature, and you'll wonder why you ever wrote any other way.

Deadly Don't #1

Passive Voice

Use Active Voice. *Teach yourself to write in active voice rather than passive voice.* Why? Because it makes the difference between strong writing and weak writing. If you need a more practical reason, here are two. Agents reject manuscripts loaded with passive voice. And *readers* find active voice engaging. Stories told in active voice carry the reader along with the action and involve the reader in the action.

The next time you pick up a good book or read an article in a leading magazine, stop and really *look* at the way the sentences are constructed. Anybody can string words together, but learning to write in active voice is an acquired skill—you get good at it by doing it over and over again.

Let's get down to business. Below are three examples of the same information rendered two different ways—in passive voice and active voice. If left untrained, most people write passively, but watch what happens when we turn that weak, limping sentence around:

PASSIVE: Two alleged drug dealers were chased by police deputies after a routine traffic stop today. One was apprehended and the other got away.

ACTIVE: Police deputies chased two alleged drug dealers today after a routine traffic stop. They apprehended one but the other got away.

In the first example, something *was done to* the drug dealers; in the second, the police *do something* to the drug dealers—chase them. The same goes for the secondary sentence describing the result of the chase.

PASSIVE: The reason she was late for work was a migraine headache that kept her up half the night, tossing and turning.

ACTIVE: A migraine headache that kept her up half the night tossing and turning made her late for work.

Again, look for a way to turn the action around so that one thing (in this case, a migraine headache) triggers something else (being late for work)—not the other way around.

PASSIVE: John and Penelope were handed an eviction notice by their landlord.

ACTIVE: The landlord handed John and Penelope an eviction notice.

Do you see the distinction? By simply turning the action around—and getting rid of weak verbs such as *was*—you create more muscular sentences. Practice writing sentences like this and before long you'll start to *think* in active voice.

I turned to YourDictionary.com[1] for more examples of passive- and active-voice sentences. The following is only a partial listing. You can find the rest on the website.

Harry ate six shrimp at dinner. (active)
At dinner, six shrimp were eaten by Harry. (passive)

Sue changed the flat tire. (active)
The flat tire was changed by Sue. (passive)

---

1   http://examples.yourdictionary.com/examples-of-active-and-passive-voice.html

The crew paved the entire stretch of highway. (active)
The entire stretch of highway was paved by the crew.
(passive)

Mom read the novel in one day. (active)
The novel was read by Mom in one day. (passive)

The critic wrote a scathing review. (active)
A scathing review was written by the critic. (passive)

I will clean the house every Saturday. (active)
The house will be cleaned by me every Saturday.
(passive)

The staff is required to watch a safety video every year.
(active)
A safety video will be watched by the staff every year.
(passive)

She faxed her application for a new job. (active)
The application for a new job was faxed by her.
(passive)

Tom painted the entire house. (active)
The entire house was painted by Tom. (passive)

The teacher always answers the students' questions.
(active)
The students' questions are always answered by the
teacher. (passive)

The choir really enjoys that piece. (active)
That piece is really enjoyed by the choir. (passive)

Who taught you to ski? (active)
By whom were you taught to ski? (passive)

The forest fire destroyed the whole suburb. (active)
The whole suburb was destroyed by the forest fire.
(passive)

The two kings are signing the treaty. (active)
The treaty is being signed by the two kings. (passive)

The cleaning crew vacuums and dusts the office every
night. (active)

Every night the office is vacuumed and dusted by the cleaning crew. (passive)

Larry generously donated money to the homeless shelter. (active)
Money was generously donated to the homeless shelter by Larry. (passive)

No one responded to my sales ad. (active)
My sales ad was not responded to by anyone. (passive)

The wedding planner is making all the reservations. (active)
All the reservations will be made by the wedding planner. (passive)

Susan will bake two dozen cupcakes for the bake sale. (active)
For the bake sale, two dozen cookies will be baked by Susan. (passive)

The science class viewed the comet. (active)
The comet was viewed by the science class. (passive)

Reading through that list might feel like doing memorization drills, or practicing your scales at the piano (anyone take piano lessons as a kid?)—but drills and scales have their purpose, and they *do* accomplish something. By the time you stagger away from the flash cards or the piano, you'll be that much more proficient.

Divine Do: Write in active voice for strong writing.

Deadly Don't #2

Weak Verbs

Here's another one Strunk & White (*The Elements of Style*) as well as your English teacher probably told you. Like the wisdom inherent in Mom's advice to eat your veggies, this method for producing great copy is so grounded in real-world results it's hard to deny.

Author Roy Peter Clark, a senior scholar with the Poynter Institute, said it better than I could, so I won't try to improve on his advice:

...Strong verbs create action, save words, and reveal the players.

President John F. Kennedy testified that his favorite book was *From Russia With Love*, the 1957 James Bond adventure by Ian Fleming. The power in Fleming's prose flows from the use of active verbs. In sentence after sentence, page after page, England's favorite secret agent, or his beautiful companion, or his villainous adversary performs the action of the verb.

Bond **climbed** the few stairs and **unlocked** his door and **locked** and **bolted** it behind him. Moonlight **filtered** through the curtains. He **walked** across and **turned on** the pink-shaded lights on the dressing-table. He **stripped** off his clothes and went into the bathroom and **stood** for a few minutes under the shower. ... He **cleaned** his teeth and **gargled** with a sharp mouthwash to get rid of the taste of the day and **turned off** the bathroom light and went back into the bedroom.

Bond **drew aside** one curtain and **opened** wide the tall windows and **stood**, **holding** the curtains open and **looking** out across the great boomerang curve of water under the riding moon. The night breeze **felt** wonderfully cool on his body. He **looked** at his watch. It said two o'clock.

Bond **gave** a shuddering yawn. He let the curtains **drop** back into place. He **bent** to

Deadly Don't #2

switch off the lights on the dressing-table. Suddenly he **stiffened** and his heart **missed** a beat...[2]

You already know, from that long list in Deadly Don't #1, that weak verbs such as *was, is,* and *will be* make for limp writing. Yes, at times you'll need to use them; just be sure it's not most of the time.

As you write, train your brain to think of strong verbs to carry your story or message across. Your readers will thank you for it—even if they can't quite pinpoint why your writing is so enjoyable.

Divine Do: Use muscular verbs in your writing.

---

2   Excerpted from *Writing Tools: 50 Essential Strategies for Every Writer* by Roy Peter Clark (New York: Little, Brown & Co., 2008). Emphasis mine.

DEADLY DON'T #3

Adjective/Adverb Overload

Ah, adjectives—those beautiful, billowy, evocative words that describe other words (nouns) and make them so much more special. Right? Yes and no. Adjectives are useful when describing a person, place, or thing, but if you string too many together, or use them too often, your writing will come across as "flabby."

Merriam-Webster reminds us, "The word *red* in 'the red car' is an adjective." This is straightforward stuff. Readers in fact prize imaginative adjectives, and today writers work very hard to mix adjectives and nouns that haven't historically been best friends.

So what's the deal with adjectives, you say? Keep reading and we'll discover the answer together.

Below are the most common adjectives used in the English language:[3]

---

3   List courtesy of http://www.englishlanguageterminology.org/

LIST OF ADJECTIVES

A-D	D-G	G-M
afraid	defeated	gorgeous
agreeable	defiant	greasy
amused	delicious	great
ancient	delightful	green
angry	depressed	grieving
annoyed	determined	grubby
anxious	dirty	grumpy
arrogant	disgusted	handsome
ashamed	disturbed	happy
average	dizzy	hard
awful	dry	harsh
bad	dull	healthy
beautiful	dusty	heavy
better	eager	helpful
big	early	helpless
bitter	elated	high
black	embarrassed	hilarious
blue	empty	hissing
boiling	encouraging	hollow
brave	energetic	homeless
breezy	enthusiastic	horrible
brief	envious	hot
bright	evil	huge
broad	excited	hungry
broken	exuberant	hurt

parts-of-speech/list-of-adjectives.htm

Deadly Don't #3

LIST OF ADJECTIVES

A-D	D-G	G-M
bumpy	faint	hushed
calm	fair	husky
charming	faithful	icy
cheerful	fantastic	ill
chilly	fast	immense
clumsy	fat	itchy
cold	few	jealous
colossal	fierce	jittery
combative	filthy	jolly
comfortable	fine	juicy
confused	flaky	kind
cooing	flat	large
cool	fluffy	late
cooperative	foolish	lazy
courageous	frail	light
crazy	frantic	little
creepy	fresh	lively
cruel	friendly	lonely
cuddly	frightened	long
curly	funny	loose
curved	fuzzy	loud
damp	gentle	lovely
dangerous	giant	low
deafening	gigantic	lucky
deep	good	magnificent

LIST OF ADJECTIVES

M-R	R-S	S-Z
mammoth	repulsive	successful
many	resonant	sweet
massive	ripe	swift
melodic	roasted	tall
melted	robust	tame
mighty	rotten	tan
miniature	rough	tart
moaning	round	tasteless
modern	sad	tasty
mute	salty	tender
mysterious	scary	tense
narrow	scattered	terrible
nasty	scrawny	testy
naughty	screeching	thirsty
nervous	selfish	thoughtful
new	shaggy	thoughtless
nice	shaky	thundering
nosy	shallow	tight
numerous	sharp	tiny
nutty	shivering	tired
obedient	short	tough
obnoxious	shrill	tricky
odd	silent	trouble
old	silky	ugliest
orange	silly	ugly

LIST OF ADJECTIVES

M-R	R-S	S-Z
ordinary	skinny	uneven
outrageous	slimy	upset
panicky	slippery	uptight
perfect	slow	vast
petite	small	victorious
plastic	smiling	vivacious
pleasant	smooth	voiceless
precious	soft	wasteful
pretty	solid	watery
prickly	sore	weak
proud	sour	weary
puny	spicy	wet
purple	splendid	whispering
purring	spotty	wicked
quaint	square	wide
quick	squealing	wide-eyed
quickest	stale	witty
quiet	steady	wonderful
rainy	steep	wooden
rapid	sticky	worried
rare	stingy	yellow
raspy	straight	young
ratty	strange	yummy
red	striped	zany
relieved	strong	

Adverbs too are a legitimate part of speech. The ones that become problematic are what I call "-ly words." Some of the most common ones are:

very	certainly
really	generally
extremely	quickly
simply	recently
nearly	usually
exactly	suddenly
particularly	eventually
clearly	directly

William Zinsser, author of *On Writing Well*, said, "Most adverbs are unnecessary." Take a gander at the list of adverbs below and it's hard to disagree with him. The list is mind-boggling. Almost every sentence that includes one of the following words could be rewritten without it.

A	C	dimly
abnormally	calmly	doubtfully
absentmindedly	carefully	dreamily
accidentally	carelessly	
acidly	cautiously	**E**
actually	certainly	easily
adventurously	cheerfully	elegantly
afterwards	clearly	energetically
almost	cleverly	enormously
always	closely	enthusiastically
angrily	coaxingly	equally
annually	colorfully	especially
anxiously	commonly	even
arrogantly	continually	evenly
awkwardly	coolly	eventually
	correctly	exactly
B	courageously	excitedly
badly	crossly	extremely
bashfully	cruelly	
beautifully	curiously	**F**
bitterly		fairly
bleakly	**D**	faithfully
blindly	daily	famously
blissfully	daintily	far
boastfully	dearly	fast
boldly	deceivingly	fatally
bravely	delightfully	ferociously
briefly	deeply	fervently
brightly	defiantly	fiercely
briskly	deliberately	fondly
broadly	delightfully	foolishly
busily	diligently	fortunately

frankly	**I**	**L**
frantically	immediately	lazily
freely	innocently	less
frenetically	inquisitively	lightly
frightfully	instantly	likely
fully	intensely	limply
furiously	intently	lively
	interestingly	loftily
G	inwardly	longingly
generally	irritably	loosely
generously		lovingly
gently	**J**	loudly
gladly	jaggedly	loyally
gleefully	jealously	
gracefully	joshingly	**M**
gratefully	joyfully	madly
greatly	joyously	majestically
greedily	jovially	meaningfully
	jubilantly	mechanically
H	judgmentally	merrily
happily	justly	miserably
hastily		mockingly
healthily	**K**	monthly
heavily	keenly	more
helpfully	kiddingly	mortally
helplessly	kindheartedly	mostly
highly	kindly	mysteriously
honestly	kissingly	
hopelessly	knavishly	**N**
hourly	knottily	naturally
hungrily	knowingly	nearly
	knowledgeably	neatly
	kookily	needily

nervously
never
nicely
noisily
not

O
obediently
obnoxiously
oddly
offensively
officially
often
only
openly
optimistically
overconfidently
owlishly

P
painfully
partially
patiently
perfectly
physically
playfully
politely
poorly
positively
potentially
powerfully
promptly
properly

punctually

Q
quaintly
quarrelsomely
queasily
queerly
questionably
questioningly
quicker
quickly
quietly
quirkily
quizzically

R
rapidly
rarely
readily
really
reassuringly
recklessly
regularly
reluctantly
repeatedly
reproachfully
restfully
righteously
rightfully
rigidly
roughly
rudely

S
sadly
safely
scarcely
scarily
searchingly
sedately
seemingly
seldom
selfishly
separately
seriously
shakily
sharply
sheepishly
shrilly
shyly
silently
sleepily
slowly
smoothly
softly
solemnly
solidly
sometimes
soon
speedily
stealthily
sternly
strictly
successfully
suddenly
surprisingly

suspiciously
sweetly
swiftly
sympathetically

T
tenderly
tensely
terribly
thankfully
thoroughly
thoughtfully
tightly
too
tremendously
triumphantly
truly
truthfully

U
ultimately
unabashedly
unaccountably
unbearably
unethically
unexpectedly
unfortunately
unimpressively
unnaturally
unnecessarily
utterly
upliftingly
upright

upside-down
upward
upwardly
urgently
usefully
uselessly
usually
utterly

V
vacantly
vaguely
vainly
valiantly
vastly
verbally
very
viciously
victoriously
violently
vivaciously
voluntarily

W
warmly
weakly
wearily
well
wetly
wholly
wildly
willfully
wisely

woefully
wonderfully
worriedly
wrongly

Y
yawningly
yearly
yearningly
yieldingly
youthfully

Z
zealously
zestfully
zestily

In this Deadly Don't we'll consider adjectives the *leaven* I mentioned earlier. A little goes a long way (after all, there's no other way to say "red car"); too many and you'll have a big mess on your hands. Some writing coaches take a more hardline approach. Zinsser considered most adjectives and adverbs "clutter." Mark Twain encouraged readers to "kill" any adjectives that survived their first drafts.

What you want to avoid is a construction that looks like this:

David was usually late for chemistry lab, but today he was very determined to be on time. The new science teacher that all the kids were talking about was said to be really kind and overwhelmingly lovely, with stunning green eyes and long, flowing, bright red hair.

As he stood outside in the sunny school courtyard, waiting impatiently to go inside, David listened to the idle chatter of his classmates, many of whom never dreamed that their words were being mentally recorded by their zealous classmate.

This may seem like an exaggerated example on my part, but a lazy writer can fall into this trap. If you write prose that's riddled with these "helping words," your manuscript will nosedive.

In an article for *Writer's Digest*, William Noble writes:

> Many inexperienced writers throw in "pretty" words to make their prose more dramatic and meaningful. But such cosmetic touch-up often turns out to be redundant or simply uninspiring. Take adverbs such as "lovingly" or "speedily" or "haltingly." They each point to some circumstance or emotion or movement, yet do they offer solid impact?
>
> ... Mark Twain had it right: "As to the Adjective: when in doubt, strike it out." The tendency is to try and beef up the noun being modified. It's human, I suppose; most of us can never be that sure we're getting our point across. Decorate that noun some more, your fragile self-confidence hears. Don't run the risk

the prose will fall flat because it isn't distinctive enough.[4]

Bottom line: watch those "pretty words." Pare down your paragraphs by taking a hard look at them.

Divine Do: Use adjectives with care; ditch most adverbs.

---

4   http://www.writersdigest.com/writing-articles/by-writing-goal/
write-first-chapter-get-started/nobles-writing-blunders-excerpt

Deadly Don't #4

"I Began to Start..."

Here we come to a phrasing habit that will mark your writing as amateurish, or at least undisciplined, quicker than you may think. So many manuscripts that cross my desk for editing fall into the same traps, and this is one pitfall I see again and again: the overuse of verb qualifiers such as "began to" or "started to" in sentences.

Other common verb qualifiers include:

sort of

tend to

in order to

kind of

must have

seem to

could have

used to

Does this mean you can never write "I began to..." or "He started to..."? Some wordsmiths take a radical approach, claiming these constructions should be outlawed except in the hands of a master. Or in realistic dialogue. I allow an exception, as you'll see below. This is an example of phrasing that gets overused to your detriment as a writer. Consider the following examples.

I began to feel goosebumps breaking out on my arms.

Edited for tightness:

Goosebumps broke out on my arms.

We started to run across the field, catching fireflies and laughing like small children.

Edited for tightness:

We ran across the field, catching fireflies and laughing like small children.

Caveat: sometimes you *need* to write "began to" or "started to" to show a progression in time (another action interrupts what was begun almost immediately) or some other development. These phrases are good and right and necessary in those instances. Just watch out for the unnecessary ones.

While editing a novel for an author client, I did a universal search for the phrases "began to" and "started to" to see how many instances might need paring. I found about one hundred of these pesky phrases. One culpable sentence read something like this: "She began to worry and started to fret about the upcoming weekend."

Taking a cue from the above scenario, let's look at a sample passage that abuses Deadly Don't #4 and then rewrite it for clarity, simplicity, and tightness. Please note that I invented this paragraph to illustrate my point for this book; it was not plucked from an anonymous writer's work.

Claire wasn't sure she could cope anymore. The pressure to keep Tom's advances at bay was starting to build, and as she thought about the upcoming weekend she began to imagine all the ways she could avoid him at the barbeque. Would he be there? Of course, she reminded herself. Wherever she went lately, he managed to be there.

If only James paid me the attention Tom does, Claire mused.

It started to drizzle outside, and as the rain picked up it began to lull her to sleep. That night she dreamed of a summer barbeque at a house she didn't recognize—and two very different men in the crowd.

Okay, now let's see how we can render this passage with a little self-editing.

Claire wasn't sure she could cope anymore. The pressure to keep Tom's advances at bay was ~~starting to~~ building fast, and as she thought about the upcoming weekend she ~~began to~~ imagined all the ways she could avoid him at the barbeque. Would he be there? Of course, she reminded herself. Wherever she went lately, he managed to be there.

If only James paid me the attention Tom does, Claire mused.

It started to drizzle outside, and as the rain picked up it ~~began to~~ lulled her to sleep. That night she dreamed of a summer barbeque at a house she didn't recognize—and two very different men in the crowd.

Notice that we didn't need to excise the phrase "started to drizzle" because it would sound awkward to write "It drizzled outside." This is an example of a time when "started to" or "began to" show a progression or development of something. You could also rewrite this clause to avoid the dreaded "started to."

A pattering sound drummed at the window, and she realized it was drizzling outside. As the rain picked up it lulled her to sleep.

Are you curious to find out what happens to Claire at the barbeque? I am too! :)

Divine Do: Eliminate "began to," "started to," and other verb qualifiers from your writing (see exception above—or get creative and rewrite).

DEADLY DON'T #5

That, That, That…

I can't stress enough how overused the word *that* is in lazy writing. Whenever I edit a manuscript for wordiness, I go after *that* like a spear-fisherman with a harpoon. Okay, fisherwoman. The same can be said for *then*.

Here's an example of lazy writing, limping along with too many *thats*:

> That winter we decided that we would walk out to the old homestead that bordered our property. For years we had known that it once belonged to a family that made its wealth in the canning business, but the Millers had fallen on hard times—like everyone else— during the Great Depression. The result was

that all but one of the original Miller clan died out without a penny to their name.

And now for a little self-editing to tighten this up:

That winter we decided ~~that we would~~ to walk out to the old homestead ~~that~~ border~~ing~~ed our property. For years we had known ~~that~~ it once belonged to a family that made its wealth in the canning business, but the Millers had fallen on hard times—like everyone else— during the Great Depression. The result: ~~was that~~ all but one of the original Miller clan died out without a penny to their name.

Better, right?

Since this Deadly Don't is so straightforward, let's move on to #6, where *that* will crop up again among other unnecessary constructions.

Divine Do: Trim excessive thats and thens from your writing.

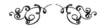

DEADLY DON'T #6

There Is/Are Overload

This Deadly Don't is a personal pet peeve, but it holds true nonetheless. Ever wade through text that reads like this?

> *There are* approximately fifty dogs *that are waiting* to be adopted at the Safe Haven Canine Rescue Shelter. Debbie Smith, director of the shelter, said *that there is* no way that all fifty dogs *will be able* to find a home before the euthanasia deadline unless the entire community gets involved.

This paragraph has a lot of bad stuff going on. Let's see what happens when we turn the action around and get rid of "there are/is" constructions, the overuse of

-ing (we'll save this Don't for a future book), and too many *thats*.

> About fifty dogs await adoption at the Safe Haven Canine Rescue Shelter. Debbie Smith, director of the shelter, said that unless the entire community gets involved, all fifty dogs will not find homes before the euthanasia deadline.

Even though this example depicts journalistic writing, the same principles hold true for fiction prose, as illustrated by Ian Fleming's famous text excerpted in Deadly Don't #2.

For this next example, we'll revisit Claire and her upcoming barbeque. Here, I've added in some "there are" phrases, extra *thats*, and a few adjectives and -ly adverbs to pad it out. I've also rendered some of the text in passive voice:

> There were days when Claire wasn't sure that she could cope anymore. The pressure to keep Tom's disgusting advances at bay was

starting to build, and as she thought about the upcoming weekend she began to imagine all the ways that she could avoid him at the barbeque. Would he be there? Of course, she reminded herself wearily. Wherever she went lately, he always managed to be there.

If only James paid me the attention Tom does, Claire mused thoughtfully.

It started to drizzle outside, and as the silvery rain picked up it began to lull her to sleep. That night her dream was of a summer barbeque at a house that she didn't recognize—and two very different men in the crowd.

Let's tighten this up, using all the lessons we've learned so far. You'll notice I've changed some of the wording to accommodate the edit:

Claire couldn't cope anymore. The pressure to keep Tom's advances at bay had built fast, and as she thought about the upcoming weekend she imagined all the ways she could avoid him at the barbeque. Would he be there? Of course, she reminded herself. Wherever she went lately, he managed to be there.

If only James paid me the attention Tom does, Claire mused.

A pattering sound drummed at the window, and she realized it was drizzling outside. As the rain picked up it lulled her to sleep. That night she dreamed of a summer barbeque at a house she didn't recognize—and two very different men in the crowd.

Do realize that as you tighten your text, it will get shorter. You may be shooting for a certain word count, hit the mark, and find out when you self-edit that you just lost five hundred words. Or three thousand words. Or fifteen thousand words, in the case of a wordy tome. I've seen it happen.

In his *Lettres Provinciales*, French philosopher and mathematician Blaise Pascal wrote: "I would have written a shorter letter, but I did not have the time." Point taken, Pascal!

Don't be shy when it comes to improving your own copy. Learn to wield the editor's "knife" yourself, and watch your words—your stories—grow more powerful in the process.

Divine Do: Rewrite (most) sentences that use "there are/is" constructions.

DEADLY DON'T #7

Telling vs. Showing

I saved the best for last. Like your English teacher's advice to write in active voice, perhaps you can also hear her or him saying, "Show, don't tell." This writing advice is so common it's become a cliché, but I'm no longer surprised to discover that many people don't know the difference between showing and telling. Let's clear this up once and for all.

Good writing is vivid writing, and if you pay attention you'll notice that the best writers—and the best books, the ones that stand the test of time—all have vivid writing. Writing that *shows* is what I call "writing with all five senses." Think of it this way: as you read along in the book, you can see the action taking place on the "silver screen" of your mind. It's like watching a movie unfold. The writer paints scenes in such a way that you are *there* with the characters (if fiction); the same can be true for nonfiction prose.

For fiction writing, this means you make the characters do the work. Make them take action. Make them speak to describe things, places, weather, whatever. Make them speak to cause action—threaten, cajole, entice, etc. Make your characters work and you'll eliminate the narrative telling.

I mentioned this earlier, but it bears repeating: if you're an aspiring writer, read as many good books as you can get your hands on. You may read a gazillion "how-to" books on writing well (including this one), but reading great writing is still the best teacher.

First let's look at some powerful, vivid writing that involves the five senses so you get a feel for what we're talking about. Count how many of the senses you experience as you read through the following excerpts. To make this fun, underline or circle every word or phrase that has to do with seeing, hearing, feeling, smelling, or tasting.

EXCERPT 1: *The Lion, the Witch, and the Wardrobe* by C.S. Lewis

(Scene: Lucy and her siblings are looking through the Professor's old house when she happens upon a huge wardrobe.)

"Nothing there!" said Peter, and they all trooped out again—all except Lucy. She stayed behind because she thought it would be worth while trying the door of the wardrobe, even though she felt almost sure that it would be locked. To her surprise it opened quite easily, and two mothballs dropped out.

Looking into the inside, she saw several coats hanging up—mostly long fur coats. There was nothing Lucy liked so much as the smell and feel of fur. She immediately stepped into the wardrobe and got in among the coats and rubbed her face against them, leaving the door open, of course, because she knew that it is very foolish to shut oneself into any wardrobe. Soon she went further in and found that there was a second row of coats hanging up behind the first one. It was almost quite dark in there and she kept her arms stretched out in front of her so as not to bump her face into the back of the wardrobe. She took a step further in—then two or three steps—always expecting to feel woodwork against the tips of her fingers. But she could not feel it.

This must be a simply enormous wardrobe! thought Lucy, going still further in and pushing the soft folds of the coats aside to make room for her. Then she noticed that there was something crunching under her feet. *I wonder is that more mothballs?* she thought, stooping down to feel it with her hands. But instead of feeling the hard, smooth wood of the floor of the wardrobe, she felt something soft and powdery and extremely cold...

Next moment she found that what was rubbing against her face and hands was no longer soft fur but something hard and rough and even prickly. "Why, it is just like branches of trees!" exclaimed Lucy. And then she saw that there was a light ahead of her; not a few inches away where the back of the wardrobe ought to have been, but a long way off. Something cold and soft was falling on her. A moment later she found that she was standing in the middle of a wood at nighttime with snow under her feet and snowflakes falling through the air.[5]

If you're like me, you found yourself right in the action with Lucy; you could feel the fur coats brushing against your cheeks, the branches scratching at your hands and face as the wardrobe contents gave way to a winter wood at night.

Consider how Lewis might have written this scene, telling instead of showing:

Lucy stayed behind to explore the wardrobe after the others had moved on to the next room. Curious, she opened the door and

---

5   C.S. Lewis, *The Lion, the Witch and the Wardrobe* (New York: HarperTrophy, 1994).

stepped inside, finding it filled with winter coats.

A second row of coats hung behind the first row, and she kept moving forward until she found herself standing in a snowy winter wood at night.

EXCERPT 2: *Home to Holly Springs* by Jan Karon

(Scene: two young boys dare each other to climb the water tower in their Southern hometown on a muggy summer night.)

The fear set into his gut the minute he climbed out Nanny Howard's window on Salem Street; as his feet hit the ground, he broke into a cold sweat. He stood behind the bushes a moment, queasy and stupefied. Then he slipped across the yard and down the bank, and raced along the silent, moonlit street like a field hare. Something small and glowing, perhaps the tip of a lighted cigarette, arced through the air as he blew by the darkened houses. His heart hammered, but he saw no one and didn't hang back.

Two dogs barked. The flashlight he carried in the pocket of his shorts banged against his leg; he took it from his pocket and held it tight. If a dog came after him, he would knock it on the head; if he was bitten, he would cross that bridge when he came to it.

He arrived at the tank, drenched with sweat and scared out of his mind that Tommy would suddenly appear from the bushes, causing him to lose it right there. In the light of the three-quarter moon, he saw Tommy; his face was as white as death. "I'm scared," said Tommy. "Don' worry, ain't nobody gon' see us." He was shaking so badly he dropped the flashlight, and had to fumble in the parched grass to find it....

Something like an electrical current shot through him when he touched the metal rung of the ladder. He drew back, then touched it again. The jolt hadn't come from special wiring to keep people from climbing to the top and writing that word; it had come from an excitement like he'd never known.[6]

Try your hand at reverse-engineering this passage to tell instead of show the action.

EXCERPT 3: *Out of the Devil's Cauldron* by John Ramirez

(Scene: a young man recalls how he grew up in the "Burnt-Out Bronx" and describes the day he sensed a pull to go deeper into spiritual darkness. Note: this true story has a happy ending.)

In the following scenario, the original manuscript read something like this:

> I lived in an area called Castle Hill in the Bronx and it was like a war zone. Gangs ruled the streets and there was always the sound

---

6   Jan Karon, *Home to Holly Springs* (New York: Viking, 2007).

of sirens. It was a dangerous place for little kids, but I had grown up there and couldn't imagine any other home, even though I longed for something better. I always had an artistic temperament.

Back then they called it the "Burnt-Out Bronx" because landlords would burn the buildings so they could collect their insurance payments on it. Everywhere you looked there was nothing but concrete and gray, ugly buildings.

By the time I was a young man I was a force to be reckoned with and I knew it. One day as I walked through the streets of Castle Hill I heard a familiar whisper in my spirit that told me to go to my aunt's house...

Tasked to find a way to make the action pop off the page, here's how I rendered it in my ghostwritten rewrite:

Shifting my feet to fight the cold, I waited at the busy crosswalk and watched my breath disperse like smoke in the wintry air. Though the temperature hovered in the low-20s, the main street through Castle Hill in the Bronx teemed with people as it always did this time of day. A cluster of little kids played at the curb, seemingly unaware of the traffic roaring past them just a few yards away. Someone leaned on their car horn and shouted obscenities at another driver. A police car zigzagged through traffic, its siren blaring and bleeping to make a path through the crush of vehicles. *Home sweet home,* I thought cynically. The light changed.

"Hey, John! What's happenin'?" a voice shouted.

I looked up to see a man I recognized from [the corner bar] near the train station, leaning against the door of the barbershop.

"Not much, man. Just keepin' it cool," I replied. We slapped hands in passing before I quickly turned the corner down a side street, not wanting to make small talk.

The cold wind whipping through Castle Hill hit me full in the face, and I turned up the collar of my wool coat. Though the winter

Deadly Don't #7

chill invigorated me physically, something nagged at my mind—a troubled feeling I couldn't shake. I glanced up to see an older Hispanic woman outside her storefront staring at me, and as I turned my dark, piercing eyes on her, fear swept over her countenance. She made the sign of the cross and hurried inside, a bell jingling in her wake.

Go to your aunt's house. The same thought I'd had earlier that day came again, this time more insistent. By now it was unmistakable: the spirits were speaking to me. Go to your aunt's house. I considered not going, but only for a minute. Changing directions, I looped back the way I'd come but avoided the main street, arriving at Aunt Maria's three-story clapboard house within minutes. I rang the doorbell and waited, then rang it again. After the third ring I decided she must not be home, but something told me to go knock on the basement door. Stepping through the chain-link gate that accessed the basement entry, I started to knock when I saw that the door was already cracked open. I walked in.[7]

EXCERPT 4: *The Great Gatsby* by F. Scott Fitzgerald

(Scene: a young man from the Midwest moves to New York to make his fortune and finds lodging in a cottage next door to a Long Island mansion. As both benign voyeur and narrator, Nick Carraway tells the tale of the enigmatic Jay Gatsby.)

There was music from my neighbor's house through the summer nights. In his blue gardens men and girls came and went like moths among the whisperings and the champagne and the stars. At high tide in the afternoon I watched his guests diving from the tower of his raft, or taking the sun on the hot sand of his beach while his motor-boats slit

---

7   John Ramirez, *Out of the Devil's Cauldron* (New York: Heaven & Earth Media, 2012).

the waters of the Sound, drawing aquaplanes over cataracts of foam. On week-ends his Rolls-Royce became an omnibus, bearing parties to and from the city between nine in the morning and long past midnight, while his station wagon scampered like a brisk yellow bug to meet all trains. And on Mondays eight servants, including an extra gardener, toiled all day with mops and scrubbing-brushes and hammers and garden-shears, repairing the ravages of the night before.[8]

EXCERPT #5: *Mrs. Dalloway* by Virginia Woolf

(Scene: an upper-class woman walks through her 1920s London neighborhood to prepare for the party she will host that evening. As she walks, she muses on the state of her life, past decisions that led to her present reality, and the inevitability of death.)

---

8   F. Scott Fitzgerald, *The Great Gatsby* (New York: Scribner, 2004).

She had the perpetual sense, as she watched the taxi cabs, of being out, out, far out to sea and alone; she always had the feeling that it was very, very, dangerous to live even one day....

Her only gift was knowing people almost by instinct, she thought, walking on. If you put her in a room with some one, up went her back like a cat's; or she purred. Devonshire House, Bath House, the house with the china cockatoo, she had seen them all lit up once; and remembered Sylvia, Fred, Sally Seton — such hosts of people; and dancing all night; and the waggons plodding past to market; and driving home across the Park. She remembered once throwing a shilling into the Serpentine. But every one remembered; what she loved was this, here, now, in front of her; the fat lady in the cab. Did it matter then, she asked herself, walking towards Bond Street, did it matter that she must inevitably cease completely; all this must go on without her; did she resent it; or did it not become consoling to believe that death ended absolutely? but that somehow in

the streets of London, on the ebb and flow
of things, here, there, she survived, Peter
survived, lived in each other, she being part,
she was positive, of the trees at home; of the
house there, ugly, rambling all to bits and
pieces as it was; part of people she had never
met; being laid out like a mist between the
people she knew best, who lifted her on their
branches as she had seen the trees lift the mist,
but it spread ever so far, her life, herself. But
what was she dreaming as she looked into
Hatchards' shop window? What was she trying
to recover? What image of white dawn in the
country, as she read in the book spread open:

Fear no more the heat o' the sun
Nor the furious winter's rages.

This late age of the world's experience
had bred in them all, all men and women, a
well of tears. Tears and sorrows; courage and
endurance; a perfectly upright and stoical
bearing. Think, for example, of the woman she
admired most, Lady Bexborough, opening the
bazaar.

. . . Oh if she could have had her life over again! she thought, stepping on to the pavement, could have looked even differently! She would have been, in the first place, dark like Lady Bexborough, with a skin of crumpled leather and beautiful eyes. She would have been, like Lady Bexborough, slow and stately; rather large; interested in politics like a man; with a country house; very dignified, very sincere. Instead of which she had a narrow pea-stick figure; a ridiculous little face, beaked like a bird's. That she held herself well was true; and had nice hands and feet; and dressed well, considering that she spent little. But often now this body she wore (she stopped to look at a Dutch picture), this body, with all its capacities, seemed nothing — nothing at all. She had the oddest sense of being herself invisible, unseen; unknown; there being no more marrying, no more having of children now, but only this astonishing and rather solemn progress with the rest of them, up Bond Street, this being Mrs. Dalloway;

not even Clarissa any more; this being Mrs. Richard Dalloway.[9]

Excerpt #6: *The Adventures of Tom Sawyer* by Mark Twain

(Scene: boy-hero Tom and Becky Thatcher, his crush, explore a cave together during a school picnic. The day swells with excitement until the two realize they are lost underground.)

[Tom and Becky] wandered down a sinuous avenue holding their candles aloft and reading the tangled web-work of names, dates, post-office addresses, and mottoes with which the rocky walls had been frescoed (in candle-smoke).

Still drifting along and talking, they scarcely noticed that they were now in a part of the cave whose walls were not frescoed....They wound this way and that, far down into the

---

9   Virginia Woolf, *Mrs. Dalloway* (1925: Harcourt, Brace & Co.).

secret depths of the cave, made another mark, and branched off in search of novelties to tell the upper world about....

Tom found a subterranean lake, shortly, which stretched its dim length away until its shape was lost in the shadows. He wanted to explore its borders, but concluded that it would be best to sit down and rest awhile, first. Now, for the first time, the deep stillness of the place laid a clammy hand upon the spirits of the children. Becky said:

"Why, I didn't notice, but it seems ever so long since I heard any of the others."

"Come to think, Becky, we are away down below them—and I don't know how far away north, or south, or east, or whichever it is. We couldn't hear them here."

Becky grew apprehensive.

"I wonder how long we've been down here, Tom? We better start back."

"Yes, I reckon we better. P'raps we better."

...They started through a corridor, and traversed it in silence a long way, glancing at each new opening, to see if there was anything familiar about the look of it; but they were all strange....

Every time Tom made an examination, Becky would watch his face for an encouraging sign, and he would say cheerily:

"Oh, it's all right. This ain't the one, but we'll come to it right away!"

But he felt less and less hopeful with each failure, and presently began to turn off into diverging avenues at sheer random, in desperate hope of finding the one that was wanted....

"All is lost!" Becky clung to his side in an anguish of fear, and tried hard to keep back the tears, but they would come....

"Listen!" said he.

Profound silence; silence so deep that even their breathings were conspicuous in the hush. Tom shouted. The call went echoing down the empty aisles and died out in the distance in a faint sound that resembled a ripple of mocking laughter.

"Oh, don't do it again, Tom, it is too horrid," said Becky.

"It is horrid, but I better, Becky; they *might* hear us, you know," and he shouted again.

The "might" was even a chillier horror than the ghostly laughter, it so confessed a perishing hope. The children stood still and listened; but there was no result. Tom turned upon the back track at once, and hurried his steps. It was but a little while before a certain indecision in his manner revealed another fearful fact to Becky—he could not find his way back![10]

I read *Tom Sawyer* in early adolescence and later saw the movie, but to this day the vividness of that scene in the cave—the one *I read in the book*—still clutches at my chest as if I were there right alongside Tom and Becky, hoping to find a way out, a way back into the light.

Divine Do: Learn to show, not tell.

---

10   Mark Twain, *The Adventures of Tom Sawyer* (Amazon Classics, 2015).

Deadly Don't #7

Now It's Your Turn

I'm going to give you a chance to do this yourself here. If possible, stop and do this short exercise right now, before you get busy and forget. When I teach writing workshops I hand out notebook paper and pens and ask the participants to write a single paragraph using vivid language. You can use a digital device if you prefer, but there's something visceral about writing the old-fashioned way for this short exercise.

A few tips will turn this into a powerful teaching moment and show you that you *can* do it:

- Think of a potent memory. It may or may not bring emotions to the surface, but it does have to be vivid.
- Childhood memories are often the most visceral— and therefore vivid.

- Rein in the knee-jerk tendency to overuse flowery adjectives; instead describe the memory with muscular verbs.
- You can use dialogue if that's a part of the memory.
- Make your paragraph no more than three or four sentences.

You'll be surprised at what you can do when you put your heart, soul, and mind into it!

_____
_____
_____
_____
_____
_____
_____
_____
_____
_____
_____
_____
_____

Deadly Don't #7

When this exercise is done in a workshop setting, I always ask brave souls to volunteer to read their paragraphs out loud. The memories that spill from their pens often move the rest of the group to tears— that's how powerful vivid writing can be.

Remember, it doesn't have to be emotionally gut-wrenching; your paragraph could recall something as simple as lying on the grass as a child and watching the clouds take strange and wonderful formations overhead.

Strange and wonderful—that about sums up what good writing, and reading, is for me. Strange, because it takes us to new places, on journeys we might otherwise never take, and ushers a cast of characters and ideas before us. Wonderful, because we come to call these characters "friends," discover ideas previously unknown to us, and for just a few hours get to peer through the eyes of the artist known as *author*.

May you always keep growing, keep learning, keep stretching as a writer. I hope one day to read your own words and get to peer through your eyes, the author.

About the Author

Angie Kiesling is a
writer, editor, author
coach, and speaker with
more than thirty years in
the publishing industry.
She has written more
than a dozen books
and edited hundreds
of manuscripts, both

fiction and nonfiction. She is the founder/owner of
The Editorial Attic, an editorial services company that
provides a full range of "wordsmithing" services to
authors. She also serves as fiction publisher for Morgan
James Publishing, a New York-based hybrid publisher.

Visit Angie at her website, www.editorialattic.com,
or contact her directly at angie@editorialattic.com. If
you'd like to schedule Angie for a writer's workshop,
please email her at angie@editorialattic.com.

Morgan James
Speakers Group

 www.TheMorganJamesSpeakersGroup.com

We connect Morgan James published authors
with live and online events and audiences who will
benefit from their expertise.

Morgan James makes all of our titles available through the Library

for All Charity Organization.

www.LibraryForAll.org